Social Media Monetization

Get Paid for Staying Online!

by

Zoya Naqvi

ALSO BY THE AUTHOR

100+ Zero Investment Profitable Business & Free Marketing Ideas

Copyright © 2022

www.thezoyanaqvi.com

All socials @thezoyanaqvi

Dedication

To everyone who is seeking ideas to start their own business, side hustles, or an additional stream of income that are less risky and only need committed action takers. This book is for you. Also, my friends motivated me to complete it and kept me accountable throughout the process.

Table of Contents

WARNING 1

Introduction 3

CHAPTER # 1 POWER OF SOCIAL MEDIA AND HOW YOU CAN TAKE ADVANTAGE OF IT 5

    Facebook – Power in Numbers 8

    Instagram–Power in Numbers 13

    LinkedIn - Power in numbers 16

    Pinterest – POWER IN NUMBERS 18

    Twitter – Power in Numbers 20

    YouTube—Power in Numbers 21

    TIKTOK - Power in Numbers 24

    Podcast – Power in number 26

    Quora - Power in numbers 28

CHAPTER # 2 FREE RESOURCES FOR LEARNING THE RIGHT & IN-DEMAND SKILLS. 31

CHAPTER # 3 THIS IS HOW YOU CAN START EARNING RIGHT NOW! 34

Personal Branding and Social Media.. 37

Conclusion... 42

About Author... 45

ACKNOWLEDGEMENTS... 47

WARNING

Read this book if you:

- Want to make money online
- Want active or passive income streams or both?
- Want to build a community
- Want to launch a business
- Want to build a personal brand
- Want to learn a skill but not sure which one
- Land a job, or work in social
- Seeking remote opportunities,
- Become an entrepreneur,
- Seeking freelance gigs,
- Aspire to become a coach, consultant, teach, or start a school

By the end of this book, you will:

- Know what you want to learn.
- How to utilize your time more efficiently and where to focus?

INTRODUCTION

As an author of the Social Media Monetization book, I have my unique journey with social media and on social media. I started using social media as a researcher and hobbyist. In 2009, I created my first business pages on all major socials and eventually started helping friends and family with their businesses, passion projects, ventures, and side hustles.

While I was a student, I instantly became a go-to person for social media and building an online presence in my social circles. Coincidently, when I started working, all of my employers gave me access to their socials. Some trained me for ad campaigns with Ad spent thousands of dollars on lead generation and engagement.

By 2017, spring to be specific, I was teaching business grads and undergrads, and social media marketing as a visiting faculty. If I revisit, the source for all my jobs, countless freelance gigs, and several other opportunities were social media. Now, when I have seen different avenues of unique uncommon opportunities online, I realized it is the perfect time for me to compile what I see, teach, and learn daily.

By 2022, I've seen multi-million online businesses working from home to dozens of employees quitting their 9-5 jobs. Not sure if they are part of the Great Resignation or not but lockdown introduced us to time freedom which is hard to trade now. Not everybody is a millionaire, but some have replaced their monthly income, build a passive source of income or personal brands that get the business. Influencer marketing is a similar but different domain because that requires a strong following, reach, or community.

However, in this book, my primary purpose is to highlight the opportunities and potential of using social media WITHOUT becoming an influencer or getting massive followers. Most of the identified monetization opportunities, if explored with the right strategy and valuable offer(s) can be potential 6-figure (USD) businesses at least. So let's get started!

CHAPTER # 1
POWER OF SOCIAL MEDIA AND HOW YOU CAN TAKE ADVANTAGE OF IT

More than half of the world now uses social media, and that translates into:

4.57 billion people use the internet and of those users,

Around 346 million new users have come online within the last 12 months.

By 2021, over 3 billion people are using social media - 3.6 billion people.

In 2020, over 3.6 billion people were using social media globally. This number is expected to increase to more or less 4.41 billion by 2025.

Imagine the potential!

No billboard, radio, film, TV ad, newspaper, magazine cover or ad, and any other source of media can give you half of this reach. And this is 100% trackable—something you still don't get with traditional media and marketing tactics. The same reason you see every marketing campaign giving equal and more importance to digital media and marketing.

There is a simple rule in the world of technology and innovation. If you do not adapt to modern trends and innovate with technology, someone will take your spot. We have seen countless examples of how a company failed to realize the need for innovation and resorted to modern trends and went on a downhill slope. This is true for every sector of technology.

Social media usage is one of the most popular online activities.

How many people are on social media?

Indulgence in Social media is one of the most popular online activities and in 2019, 79 percent of the population in the United States had a social networking profile, representing a two percent increase from the 77 percent usage reached in the previous year.

Social Media Analytics Market Worth $3.58 Billion in 2020; Expected to Reach $15.57 Billion by 2025

Facebook is the most popular social media platform with 3.5 billion Social media users worldwide. 90.4% of Millennials,

77.5% of Generation X and 48.2% of Baby Boomers are active social media users.

Users spend an average of 3 hours per day on social networks and messaging.

Why only Social Media Marketing?

There are over 100 social networking sites, but we will focus on the industry leaders only. I intend to sum up everything I have gained so far as a lifelong student and researcher.

Well, this has to be my favorite. My friends knew it since 2009 when I started my Facebook page and grew 2000+ with a friend organically. My students know it because I still help them with SMM after 3 years of them graduating. My colleagues know because I had been taking classes forever and bugging them with questions. If you want to learn all about social media marketing today, I won't recommend that. I did and I am still learning every day with every update. Pick one platform and cash it. Why?

How to earn through SMM platforms?

I wish I could teach you how to utilize each platform as well. But you can YouTube, Google, and sign up for free/paid courses. For me, I wish I had one place to learn from or one person who could spoon-feed me because there are countless sources and what you acquire is a piece of scattered information. Knowledge is power any day, which is why I'm compiling everything here to help you all navigate your journey.

What can we do after learning about social media?

- You can get a job—every business has at least 1 social media page.
- Take freelance jobs.
- Start your own SMM agency based on one platform or all.
- Start teaching.
- Start a school.
- Sell courses for each skill or method you learned.

FACEBOOK – POWER IN NUMBERS

Facebook is the third-most visited online platform; second-most downloaded app; has 2.74 billion monthly active users that makes 59% of the world's online population

Around 57% are male and almost 43% are female Facebook users.

Facebook Users tend to spend at least 34 minutes daily on average. 79.9% of users access Facebook on a mobile device

36% get news from Facebook while 45% of new-music seekers discover new music on Facebook

500 million people use Facebook Stories daily

Billion People use Facebook Messenger, and 1.8 billion people use Facebook Groups

33% biz is based in urban businesses, and 25% are based in rural areas.

48.5% of B2B decision-makers use Facebook for research

The average Facebook Page shares 1.55 posts per day, 55.6% of them are photos, 18.5% links, 22.2% are videos, and just 3.6% are simple status updates.

How to earn through Facebook?

The Facebook business encourages its users to pay for each post therefore, the room to grow organically is not too much. However, if you are doing paid marketing, Facebook Marketing is GOLDMINE. How you can take advantage of millions of active users online:

Help businesses generate leads through paid or organic methods.

Manage Facebook pages for others—post content.

Run ads for businesses.

Design content for social media pages.

Write engaging captions and become a copywriter.

Start a blog on a business page and grow your own audience. Meme page anyone? News, views, reviews, write or put a video. Once you have to build your voice, you can take paid collaborations, and shoutouts for brands, and don't forget small businesses.

Help businesses or individuals grow their followers.

Start a shop using the Facebook shop feature. Sell stuff. Promote for affiliate or marketing commission.

Generate traffic for websites. Paid or Free both.

Sell something, a product or service of your own. Through a group page, run ads.

Ever seen the ads for something you saw on a website? That's Pixel tracking you on your Facebook feed. Help businesses with Pixel Marketing.

Become a Facebook expert, teach, consult, or coach.

Start an NGO if you love volunteer work. Build it, volunteers, onboard, and you will start getting funds after social proof. You can enjoy what you do, earn, hire people, and generate an economy.

You can now monetize your articles and videos on Facebook similar to YouTube and Google AdSense.

Good at building pages? Sell them after growing them.

As a Facebook manager and Facebook Marketer, you can offer your services or start your agency and get on board with more than one client.

Build Facebook Messenger Chabot

Host Webinar using Facebook Events

Source candidates using the Facebook jobs tool.

Become a mentor and guide someone. It is an official FREE volunteer program launched by Facebook. They handpicked me in 2018 for this. You can create a page and do the same, but get paid for it. Make it clear.

Content Creator? Facebook is now paying you through In-stream video ads,

Brand partnerships.

Memberships subscriptions

Become an Expert in a Group

How?

Help people genuinely for free. Eventually, switch to paid help if you offer those services.

Utilize Groups: Build an ORGANIC group for helping people only! Use that traffic for your YouTube or blog. Start training, and become an authority with time and expertise.

Start a premium group. Teach people or share your freebies with them.

Manage communities aka groups of various companies. Get paid! You will have to reply promptly to the queries and comments on posts.

Buy And Sell Groups—offer others your space to sell or buy from your group.

Promote Products and Services in a group and earn a commission or marketing fee for that.

Instream Videos

How do In-stream videos work?

- You must have a Facebook business page that has 1000 followers.
- You require 30,000 1-minute views on your videos in the last 60 days that are a minimum of 3 minutes long.
- You must meet their policy guidelines.

How do Brand Collaborations work?

For Facebook's official brand partnership program eligibility, you must have at least:

- 1000 followers on your Facebook Business page
- 180,000 minutes of total watch time OR 15,000 post engagements on all your videos in the last 2 months.

Well, until you meet these criteria, or even if you don't, you're free to collaborate on a sponsored deal yourself - with anyone else.

How do Fan Subscriptions work?

Content creators have been doing fan subscriptions for years with the help of other platforms such as Patreon), but this is something relatively new to Facebook. This program is presently run by invitations only.

Here's how Facebook states it:

- Create a subscription for your Facebook Page and make money through the monthly subscription fee.
- Select a suitable monthly plan, offer some exclusive benefits, and build a community of people who would subscribe to this to support you.

Instagram—Power in Numbers

About 90% of accounts on Instagram follow businesses, mostly retail brands.

There are about 60% of Instagram users busy discovering new products on the platform.

Facial images enjoy more likes out of the daily 4.2 billion likes given by Instagram users.

One-third of the people search for and buy mobile phones through Instagram.

Over two million advertisements per month are there on Instagram.

High engagement rates are there in the higher education industries.

Instagram turns out to be the widely chosen collaboration platform for 80% of influencers.

How to earn through Instagram?

Pick a niche, grow followers(optional), build a community rather, and start

1. Blogging and sharing your views.
2. Diving into Influencer Marketing.
3. Selling your services. Don't have one? Learn a new skill.
4. Launch your shop and utilize it as e-commerce.
5. Don't have the investment to start a retail business? Affiliate, Dropshipping, there are plenty of ways, you just need the right frame of mind to do it.

6. Collaborate with brands as content creators, endorse local businesses, or run a community - paid!
7. Generate leads for other businesses by lending your space.
8. If you have grown your account: flip that if you don't want to become an influencer, launch a product, or offer paid services.
9. If you think you've learned everything, start teaching, and become a consultant. Help others grow through your expertise. Make success plans for others.
10. Start your own Instagram agency.
11. Become an Instagram content or growth strategist or do hashtag research for brands. You can pick one task and build an empire.

Instagram is the most engaging visual medium, take advantage of that as a photographer, actor, designer, visual artist, makeup artist, stylist, filmmaker, or anything that involves visuals. Don't want to show your face or do you prefer writing? Start reviewing stuff, could be a book or whatever you look at. Ironically, everything involves a visual connection. Would you take medicine from a doctor you have never seen? Seeing is believing. 32% of users are aged between 18 and 24 and 33% are aged between 25 and 34.

Learn your strengths and capitalize on them by bringing the visual side to them. If you have services, tell your story, and share your customer's experience, there are countless ways to utilize this space and make your niche.

Unfortunately, Instagram's organic growth has become a challenge for many since 2020. Similar to Facebook it encourages people to spend on paid marketing. Those who do how to play with paid marketing - LOVE it. The results are just amazing IF you know how to do it. However, there are organic ways to grow on Instagram, I raised half a dozen as a hobby and helped a few brands but now it's business and you have to learn how HASHTAGS works.

Not sure where to start? Get in touch. I might help you. Or join my community - it's FREE!

LinkedIn - Power in Numbers

LinkedIn has:

There are 30 million companies registered on LinkedIn, with 61 million people using the platform as senior influencers.

4 out of 5 LinkedIn users make business decisions, which puts around 40 million users in decision-making sections.

Over 0.5 billion professionals are there on LinkedIn, making it the most widely used social media platform among 500 companies.

The ratio of content distribution between B2B marketers is 97%, with 94% of other marketers who distribute the content. B2B gets 80% leads from LinkedIn, which is more insane than Facebook and Twitter, which give 7% and 13% respectively. LinkedIn is the most recommended platform for lead generating, as 79% of B2B marketers prefer it. 59% of B2B marketers stated they make their business leads through LinkedIn.

How to earn through LinkedIn?

By definition, LinkedIn is a professional networking site where job-seekers connect with employers and so on. The brighter side, that only LinkedIn peeps know is,

1. LinkedIn is a goldmine for freelancers, and people who prefer working on projects only instead of full-time jobs.
2. Generate leads which makes it a great platform for B2B (business-to-business) and B2C(Business-to-clients)
3. LinkedIn groups are great tools for earning gigs and jobs (of course). Full of opportunities, irrespective of where you live.

4. Organic growth - grow your brand, business page, blog, or anything you are good at.
5. Want to hire? Save a great deal of money and recruit here online.
6. Run ads for clients, and manage their business accounts.
7. Become a social media recruiter, source candidates for companies, source clients or businesses for companies, and serve them warm or cold leads.
8. Reach out to Fortune 500 companies' management or any company you want to work with – for business or employment.
9. Give paid reviews, help people develop their profiles, and appear in searches to get their dream jobs.
10. Looking for a job? Make sure your profile is optimized and mentioned in your BIO. Get in touch. Find me on LinkedIn. Maybe I can help you!
11. Start a membership group.

Apply anywhere in the world. But it won't let you if you don't meet the criteria. Great place for authors, writers, freelancers, entrepreneurs, B2B and B2C sales, HR, and recruitment agencies. If you never knew this, now you have power (read: knowledge).

PINTEREST – POWER IN NUMBERS

With over 400 million monthly users, Pinterest stands in the third spot after Google and YouTube.

Homes with high income use Pinterest twice than homes with low income.

The average price of sales that people get through Pinterest is $50.

Out of 100%, of Pinterest users scrolling through products, 73% purchase an item they see.

47% of the users take it as a source of creating plans for the future, 89% call it a source of inspiration for them, and 97% of the searches are for products that don't come under a famous brand name.

Not using faces in brand images will give it 23% more pins than images having faces. Therefore, you'll see around 20% or fewer images that have faces.

Services related to home decor and beauty & fashion are likely to enjoy more sales on Pinterest.

80% of the pins on Pinterest are re-pinned. For gathering around 50% of engagement, one pin might take 3 and a half months.

How to earn through Pinterest?

Pinterest is another search engine, people looking for ideas, inspiration or DIYs go to Instagram and find smarter ideas there. It has 433 million monthly active users by July 2022, utilize that place, it is free, get hired, get paid, and sell your product or service. How?

Follow what you love, post consistently about it, make sure it is visually rich, and inspire something. Build an audience out of it, and sell something to them.

Promote a company, and get its sponsored sponsorship.

Generate traffic for your affiliate products.

Utilize search engine optimization (SEO) strategies to get noticed on Pinterest. Drive that traffic on your website and earn.

Launch your brand, and sell your products on Pinterest.

Design Pinterest growth strategies for businesses.

Teach Pinterest marketing.

Manage Pinterest accounts for others.

Promote ads for other businesses, manage their accounts, and get paid.

If you know how to grow a Pinterest audience, flip it and turn it into a business.

TWITTER – POWER IN NUMBERS

Around 80% of people on Twitter are youngsters having a handsome income, property, and lifestyle.

Compared to other social media platforms, 38% of users will love sharing their views about brands and products.

85% of businesses prefer Twitter for providing an active customer support service.

How to earn through Twitter?

1. Get paid per tweet after reaching a certain amount of audience.
2. Become a meme strategist, if you are good at it.
3. Promote Affiliate Products on Twitter
4. Generate Traffic for Your Website
5. Generate leads for other businesses. Charge per lead.
6. Create Twitter Ads for clients as a freelancer.
7. Manage Twitter accounts and design Twitter growth strategies for clients.
8. If you know how to grow a Twitter audience, start flipping it. Make it your business.
9. Monetize Your Twitter Presence through Twitter Media Studio

YOUTUBE—POWER IN NUMBERS

After Google, YouTube holds the title of the world's second-largest, second most visited, and second highest-ranked search engine & website.

90% of YouTube users love exploring information about new companies or newly launched products. A tutorial video on YouTube will have three times more traffic than a website with written instructions.

48% of B2B buyers watch YouTube videos through their smartphones.

The recommendation of B2B marketers has put YouTube in 4th place for being the most valuable social media platform.

92% are the influencers responsible for uploading branded videos on YouTube.

About 51% of B2B and B2C use YouTube for running marketing ads. These video ads will make around 46% of B2B technology buyers purchase the products.

How to earn through YouTube?

YouTube has officially become the largest search engine. Hint? Start with something people are already searching for. YouTube is a global phenomenon and social powerhouse.

Criteria?

As of now, you need 1000 subscribers and 4000 hours of watch time to start your monetization. Abide by the terms and conditions and start filming your podcast if you want. Post them here as well, or shoot something else that people are looking for. The only key to success on YouTube? More than your niche, YouTube SEO helps you rank above everyone else, with attractive covers, communication, expensive gear, and whatnot - make sure you are consistent. I know some YouTubers who got a few views and went viral at their 600th post. Don't lose hope!

Apply for the YouTube Partner Program.

There are 2 further YouTube Programs: A premium program that is Subscription-based, similar to Facebook where you run a membership-based channel.

Membership channels can be a bit tricky if you don't have a massive audience. Its criteria are challenging as compared to the popular one. So, you can earn through selling membership yourself to individuals and sharing customized link.

Earn through Affiliate programs.

Collaborate with brands before you qualify for the YouTube Partner Program.

Launch a course, and teach what you are good at.

Launch a series, do what you love ONLY, so you don't leave it halfway.

Ask your subscribers to fund you. They do. If you have a community and share something valuable. Why wouldn't they?

Master YouTube SEO. Offer your paid services to others.

Teach YouTube or through YouTube. The open/public links will allow you to get more traffic. You can also customize links (private) for your students only.

Use it for generating traffic on your blog, or affiliate products.

Explore YouTube Red Subscribers if that suits you. It offers viewers to watch ad-free content at $9.99.

By using ad monetization, affiliate links, and selling sponsored placements in your videos, you can maximize your revenue potential. On YouTube, you can make money from ads on a CPM, CPV, and CPC basis. With cost per impression (CPM), a typical YouTuber makes $7.60 per 1,000 views. Nonetheless, by Google policy, creators get 55% of earnings accrued from advertisements while Google keeps 45%.

TIKTOK - POWER IN NUMBERS

Tiktok has been downloaded over 2 billion times so far.

An average Tik Tok user spends 89 minutes/day on the app, according to Music Business Worldwide.

By 2021, there were 14.43 million active daily TikTok users on Android App. (Hootsuite, Statista,)

Younger users aged between 4 and 15 spend almost 80 minutes a day on Tiktok. (Qustodio)

As per a leaked TikTok deck, an average Tiktok user checks the app more or less 19 times a day. (Music Business Worldwide)

TikTok Android users now spend more time watching content on TikTok than on YouTube. (App Annie)

TikTok has the highest reach for Gen Z users, which translates into 17.9% of male users and 25% of female tiktokers aged 18-24.

As per AppAnnie, TikTok ranks as the #1 app for driving consumer spending, overtaking Tinder in the first spot.

TikTok has been downloaded over 3 billion x making it the 6th most-used social platform globally.

How to earn from TikTok

- TikTok offers five tiers of advertising for big brands. A branded hashtag is one challenge, which reportedly costs $150,000 a day.
- To earn directly from TikTok, the user must be a minimum of 18 years (or older) and must have at least 10k followers, and a

minimum of 100,000 views on their video(s) in the last 1 month. This is the threshold to apply for TikTok's Creator Fund using the app.
- TikTok Influencers with 2.5m or more followers conventionally charge around $600-$1000 for one post while Instagram Influencers with 10,000-20,000 followers charge up to $100-$200 for one post (Telegraph, 2019)
- TikTok launched a $1 Billion Creator Fund to support and encourage content creators. Through this, TikTok will directly pay to strengthen its relationship with content creators and influencers.
- Become a TikTok Influencer by creating content that resonates with the masses.
- Grow and Sell TikTok Accounts.
- Get Sponsorships/Brand deals.
- Sell Your Own Products for passive income.
- Collect Donations.
- Become a TikTok Consultant.
- Start A TikTok Talent Management Agency.

Podcast – Power in Number

Comedy is the most in-demand genre, subsequent to educational and information/news podcasts.

Podcast listeners tend to follow brands and companies on social media.

The podcast audience is more active on several social media platforms. That makes 94% of them who are active on one SM channel vs 81% of the rest of the population.

69% of podcast listeners agreed that podcast ads are aware of new services or products.

How to earn through Podcast?

If you don't know any skills and don't know where to start, I am sure you know how to strike a conversation. The good news for introverts, you can write down and discuss your questions with your interviewee and let them answer. You won't be talking too much if you interview someone.

Make sure you don't exceed 20-30 minutes. If you are an extrovert, what could be better than this than talking about something you love? Regardless of your personality type, if you know something, or learned something today or with time, start with once a week and you will have 52 episodes by the end of this year. Start recording now. Share with your friends and family, take their feedback, and utilize social media to your advantage. According to Statistica, 332.2 million people are listening to podcasts.

How Much Money Do Podcasts Make?

Popular names get immense amounts of listeners which help them generate significant ad revenue in return as revenue.

As per AdvertiseCast, an average 30-second cost per 1000 listeners, i.e. CPM pays around $18, whereas CPM per 60-second is $25.

So how do small podcasts generate money?

Some examples:

The Last Podcast on the Left managed to generate about $57,000 a month only via Patreon. Besides that, they do live shows in several cities and sell shirts.

The Bowery Boys podcasts about New York City's history make about $3,800 a month via Patreon.

So technically podcasts work as a lead magnet for most businesses.

QUORA - POWER IN NUMBERS

When consulting the internet for queries, people find it useful to go through Quora. It has been helping internet users by answering almost every question.

Quora is worth $2 Billion, having information about 400,000 versatile topics.

There are over 300 million monthly users on Quora, out of which, Americans and Indians are 35% and 23% respectively. The percentage of Quora Ads for B2C and B2B is 40% and 60% respectively.

37% of the users on Quora have the role of management.

Compared to LinkedIn, the number of adults on Quora is twice.

Those businesses that use Quora Ads get four times more conversions than other platforms.

Young people enjoying a reasonable income of over $100,000 use Quora for collecting information.

When browsing queries on search engines, 63% of users click on Quora to get the solution.

Compared to other popular online platforms, Quora has the highest percentage of 18+ users.

How to monetize Quora?

Describe Your Skills:

If you are a master of any skill, start writing about it on Quora. If you are a content writer who knows how to write unique and plagiarism-free content, you can share your tips on Quora. You might think that what would be the advantage of describing this? Disclosing your knowledge about your skill will increase your credibility.

1. Add your blog links: When you notice the number of users growing, it is time for you to add links to your Quora Space. It will make you hook the attention of your targeted audience. Understand what they want to read and provide them with well-crafted content. It will result in a long-term readership connection.
2. Networking: You are not the only one working in your niche. Look for people who are offering the best services in your niche. Interact with them to learn new strategies. If you managed to build a powerful network with a team of experts, you would more likely increase your success rate than your competitors.
3. Profile Building: 700 million page views per month is what Quora enjoys every month. It hooks around 72% of traffic from search engines. You can focus on your credibility and increase your followers on Quora and other social media profiles. You might struggle to find followers on Quora, but it will increase with time. Once you have some followers, they'll vote for every answer you write. It will make new users trust you provide the most accurate information. This step will take you to progress and emerge as a successful individual.

Quora Space Partner Program

The "Space Updates" program states:

- Wait for a few weeks as everyone will be able to create a free Space on Quora.
- Quora will use ads to make the Quora spaces better than before. Besides it, the revenue sharing program has also started.

CHAPTER # 2
FREE RESOURCES FOR LEARNING THE RIGHT & IN-DEMAND SKILLS.

For making money on social media, you either need to have a service or a product. You can check my book 100+ Zero Investment Profitable Business & Marketing Ideas for more ideas. Moreover, having some marketing or digital skills can be your competitive advantage and increase your chances of success.

So I'm enlisting some free resources that you should take advantage of. That doesn't change the fact that YouTube and Google should be your best friends in this process and will make the journey smoother. Here you go!

Free Resources for learning the skills.

Google Garage has all the free courses on Digital Marketing.

Udemy and **Coursera** have a free filter. Select that and you are good to go.

Free trails:

Skillshare, Facebook Education, LinkedIn, and Edx.

You can watch content and courses on YouTube for:

    a. Social media:

Gary V, Rachel Pederson, Latasha James, Dan Lok.

b. SEO and Affiliate Marketing

Neil Patel, Matt Digity, Brain Dean (Backlinko), Income School,

c. YouTube

Creator Suite by Youtube, Salma Jafri, Vanessa Lau, Gillian Perkins.

d. Instagram

Jasmine Star, Founder Magazine, and all of the above.

These resources have helped me a lot, though I never shy away from investing in myself or asking for help, and clarifying my doubts, whether it is a paid course or a coaching program.

Pro-tip: Investing in yourself is something you will never regret in life.

Learn ONLY what resonates with you. Focus on one thing instead of getting distracted by shiny object syndrome. You will feel exhausted and will eventually notice the more attention you give to one niche/subject the more it grows.

I'm glad you have read this far, I think I should suggest some ideas for you to utilize your SM earning game through more than one business model.

CHAPTER # 3
THIS IS HOW YOU CAN START EARNING RIGHT NOW!

Affiliate Marketing and Platforms

Competing in broad niche markets is entirely possible, but competing in narrow, super-focused niches is easier and can be more profitable.

Profitable Industries to consider:

1. Languages & Translation

Market Worth: Us$43 Billion per Year

2. The Pet Niche Is Huge

$100 per Day for Reliable Pet Sitters

Market Value: $66.75 Billion per Year

3. Prepping

Market Value: Us$16 Billion – Us$37 Billion per Year

4. Relationships & Dating

Market Value: Us$2.5 Billion

5. Personal Finance

Market Value: US 17 Billion per Year

6. Home Security

Market Value: Us$51 Billion per Year

7. Babies

Market Value: Us$18 Billion per Year

8. Weight Loss Market

Market Value: Us$66 Billion per Year

9. Learning Music

Market Value: Us$6 Billion per Year

10. Electronic Entertainment

Market Value: Us$65 Billion per Year

Affiliate programs that don't require massive following/traffic:

1. Amazon

2. Godaddy

3. Bluehost

4. Flash deal

5. Get a response.

How to reach out to brands for collaborations

Create your social media influence.

Build your community.

Niche down – don't keep it generic like entrepreneur or lifestyle. Narrow down. More. Niche-niche-niche down.

Nano influencers who have 10k or fewer followers are more in demand in coming years than someone with 100k. Why?

Who would you go to if you have to QUICKLY get a flared pair of jeans?

Most likely a shop you already know has it and doesn't have hassle.

Would you hop from one shop to another in a mall if you are short on time?

Similarly, the brands want to reach out to an audience that is small yet more relevant than reaching the masses and not converting the promotions into sales.

Create your media kit, and make sure you have earned some numbers in the insights of your platform.

Highlight the number of followers and engagement on average,

Mention your previous collaborations (if any), your niche, screenshots of the insights, and your profile.

Make sure you have your own brand colors.

Create a minimal-themed media kit with flawless content in it.

Reach out to potential collaborations.

Send a short email showing your interest in your media kit. Tell them the reasons they should work with you.

Please don't lose hope after sending a couple of emails/DM outreach.

Repeat the process and reach out to a maximum number of brands that you could work with based on the relevancy between you and their brand.

PERSONAL BRANDING AND SOCIAL MEDIA

We all have our social media accounts that we use for staying in touch with friends and family. Sometimes for staying on top of news, memes, or the latest happenings in the world generally. We follow our favorite celebrities, now influencers, or businesses that we support. Most of us share our controversial opinions on Twitter or Facebook or comment if we see something that doesn't sit well with us.

How about we start using at least one platform for building our Personal brand that highlights our strengths and how people can work or collaborate with us. The business model for Personal Brands is quite similar to Influencer Marketing or Content Creators who have massive followings. However, there are some key differentiators that set Personal Brand apart and make them instant authority.

1. Personal Brands don't need thousands of followers to monetize their presence.
2. They work on building community, not following.
3. They share valuable, helpful educational or informative content.
4. Content forms could be text, Lives, videos, training, and pictorial forms.
5. Networking is an integral part of building a Personal Brand.
6. Personal Brands don't have to wait for brands to collaborate or get money.
7. They have at least one offer/service.

8. Usually, high tickets offer $1k-$2k minimum so they only need 3-6 clients to make 6-figures a year.
9. 1 skill + 1 social media platform + 1 offer is more than enough to make you a millionaire using your profile leveraging your Personal Brand.
10. Their Personal Profile eventually becomes a brand story when they start documenting their journey in establishing their brand story.

Best part of building a Personal Brand:

- You stay on top of people's minds as a friend but are known for your expertise.
- You get paid for what you are good at, not for what you are supposed to do.
- You create your job description. It's a constant learning process, so you are forced to evolve.
- You don't have to copy anyone, your entire marketing strategy is BEING YOU.
- Your brand voice, tone, and lingo are how you want to be known.
- You create the perception that people buy and eventually invest.
- You can start multiple businesses, offer different services, and change the game because you're not afraid of getting lost in business names and logos. There can be millions of Zoya but people who know me would think of me first.

- Your name is synonymous with what you do: Personal Branding Coach? Zoya can help you.
- You get referrals and recommendations without asking for them.
- It is equally important for students and 9-5 employees, so you can attract work, job, and collaboration opportunities.

In case you don't know, I'm a Personal Branding and Organic Visibility Coach. That's what I teach and that's what I do for a living.

Best Platforms to build your Personal Brand:

1. Facebook

2. LinkedIn

3. Instagram

4. Tiktok YouTube

Pick one platform, start posting valuable content, and connect with like-minded people and people who could be interested in your services. Don't get stuck in branded content, or fancy vocabulary, just get clear on what you want and break it down into daily and weekly goals so you can ultimately monetize that.

Oh, and don't forget to show your face. To make it personal, your face sets you apart in the crowd, and your voice whether in text format, audio or video gets you recognized online.

Keep going, the process can be slow but the results are certain.

Free and Paid Tools for Social Media Growth, Management, and Business.

Google Analytics - Measure the value of social media as a channel by analyzing conversions and e-commerce transactions and Find social networks and communities where people are interacting with your content.

Hootsuite - Overview of key metric

Sprout Social - for seeing analytics.

Buffer - for managing content.

LastPass - for password sharing.

Creator Suite or Business Suite by Facebook: Managing content.

Canva: For designing pretty posts.

Tiktok, ***Camtasia*** and ***Inshot*** for Video content

Optimization Tools: Keyword Planner for SMO and SEO.

SEO Tools: Moz, SEM Rush, Ahref

Trello and ***Asana*** for Project Management

All the tools from ***Google Suite***.

Grammarly and ***Prowriting*** for polishing your content.

BuzzSumo, Answerthepublic, and Twitter Trends for social updates.

Mailchimp, ***MailerLite***, ***GrooveFunnels*** for landing pages, newsletter, email marketing, generating leads, etc.

Fiverr, ***Upwork***, ***Freelancer***, for gigs and outsourcing any work.

TubeBuddy and ***VidQ*** for YouTube analytics and content Strategy.

Calendly for booking meetings.

MemberVault, ***Patreon***, ***Thinkific***, for selling courses, memberships, paid community of learners, and trainers/teachers.

Card, ***Canva***, and ***Google sites*** for websites without domain and hosting.

Wix, Squarespace, WordPress for free websites.

Medium, ***Blogspot***, for blogging.

Conclusion

This book Social Media Monetization (Get paid for staying online) is an effort to invite those friends who use social media but not for freelancing, building Personal brands, networking with the right people, and getting known for what we love doing. Growing Social Media is one piece of the puzzle but getting business out of it is not something many are doing. That's where you can find a skill that you want to become an expert at and monetize that.

Action plan for you:

- Learn a skill or become an expert if you are already skilled.

- Start your venture on any of the said platforms.

- Build a social media

- Build a community/following that is genuinely interested in it.

- Pick any or more of these strategies.

- Follow YouTubers and research your idea on Google

- Study case studies (people doing similar stuff) to see what works and what does not work.

- Take a certification or course to upgrade your knowledge - Start documenting your journey.

- Share your venture with people.

Ask for help!

Working with coaches and consultants is not mandatory or the only way to success. It's a privilege and smart way to have someone who is ahead of you in your journey to guide you at every step. Tag along with a senior.

Consultant can give you a roadmap that you will have to follow. Coaches will hold your hand to take you to your desired destination. Both reduce the chances of failure and increase the possibility of getting to your destination sooner.

If hiring a coach or consultant is not feasible for you at this point in time, YouTube is a great place to start researching or request someone to barter their services/skills against yours.

Final word

Change your algorithms to change your life. You cannot watch cat videos, memes, and Netflix and expect a successful business or profitable venture.

Compartmentalize - 80-20 rule. Make sure your maximum attention is on your venture if you want maximum returns eventually. You have to get serious before you expect someone else to take you and your ideas seriously.

Unfollow, delete, block, or whatever you think you can to train your algorithm that you are not interested in food, shopping, or entertainment ads. You will stop seeing that after a while. The same goes for the people you follow online because we are an average of 6 people we surround ourselves with. You have to hang out with like-minded people and people with a progressive approach to life to eventually become one of them. Avoid negativity, gossip, and controversial or subject matters that invite conflicting debates online and offline.

If you liked the book and found something helpful, please share it with someone who you think would find it valuable. Also, I would appreciate it if you could leave a review on Amazon.

ABOUT AUTHOR

Personal Branding Coach / Organic Marketing & Visibility Strategist / Author

When Zoya is not writing or working on her passion projects and personal development in her favorite coffee shop, you can find her journaling, learning interesting stuff, and binge watching YouTube or Netflix.

On Tuesday night you can find her doing yoga, in the middle of the day taking long peaceful walks, sipping tea in 100F and she will not compromise on her uninterrupted sleep. Don't be shocked if you see her making friends in a waiting lounge because her friendly nature wins her friends everywhere more than she could keep up with.

As an Enneagram 7 and Aries, her self-assured, slightly loud, and open-minded personality intimidates some and attracts secure, ambitious, and confident people. Still, she has a small circle of amazing friends. If something or someone doesn't align with her, you won't see her around again.

Her threshold to tolerate something that costs her peace has been too low since she was a kid. She has changed her entire lifestyle multiple times, rebuilt her career, network, and everything she thought doesn't go with where she sees herself in the future.

Her family has always been the most important part of her life until her passion projects and the minute her passion became her profession took over. Even though she's competitive, her attention span is less, and she knows it, so she keeps things interesting with new hobbies and religiously believes in discipline. In the middle of the pandemic, she was juggling painting classes, writing her books, doing some certifications and yoga all while managing her remote job, road trips, and business mentorship programs she signed up for.

Get in touch with Zoya:

Website: https://www.thezoyanaqvi.com/

All socials: @thezoyanaqvi

Join her community on Facebook exclusively for the readers:

Free Marketing Ideas | Digital Marketing | Monetization | Biz Ideas

ACKNOWLEDGEMENTS

I would like to thank Ms. Nagwa Malik, who is an author, and was our Scriptwriting teacher while I was doing my Masters in Filmmaking. I never knew I would be writing books but even then my inclination was towards digital media and marketing. That was the reason Ms. Nagwa, who is always writing books and releasing series, involved me in her marketing plans.

I had been hanging out with authors and best-selling authors online for almost a decade. That's where I learned that the real OG's don't have time to pinpoint or cringe over spelling or grammatical mistakes. It comes from a place of "a king with partial vision in a kingdom of blind people".

She and all the authors made it look so easy which is far from the truth. Writing a book and series is nerve-wracking and got on my nerves. I've been sitting on this idea since 2018 summers, due to work commitments and other passion projects, it almost got abandoned multiple times. I would like to thank ALL the people who held me accountable, because the book(s) are finally here. :)

Special mention to Sherbano for supporting me at every single step, Zaeema for keeping me accountable and eventually recording the audiobooks as Zoya, and Maryam Nawaz, again for not only making it look so easy but giving me simple tips and tricks that kept the needle moving.

Almighty, of course, for enabling me with ALL the resources and support through and through that it became a series. *pinch me* My family, even though they don't comprehend the point behind the all-nighters and hard work I put into my unconventional projects. I understand my WHY which is to be as resourceful as possible because it is a calling, not a conference call so it is not supposed to make sense. I follow my mission and purpose without making sense to anyone. I look forward to connecting with my books' readers on social media.

I invite all of my book readers to a Facebook group so we can connect and co-create something substantial because I am sure this will attract like-minded and progressive-minded people only.

Lets hang out in this Facebook community:

Free Marketing Ideas | Digital Marketing | Monetization | Biz Ideas and post *"No-Cost Digital Products"* to get the list I have exclusively curated for my readers.

I look forward to connecting with you @thezoyanaqvi and reading your feedback. If you found this book helpful for yourself or someone you know - do share with them and kindly leave a review on Amazon.

That would mean the world to me.

Thanks for your support!

www.ingramcontent.com/pod-product-compliance
Lightning Source LLC
Chambersburg PA
CBHW050313220526
45465CB00005B/1965